A+ books

WORLD OF COLORS

Russia in Colors

by Catherine Ipcizade

Consultant: Eliot Borenstein, Chair
Russian and Slavic Studies
New York University

Capstone press

Mankato, Minnesota

A **brown** bear splashes in the river to catch a fish. The brown bear is the national animal of Russia. Brown bears live all over Russia. They eat fish, plants, and fruit. The brown bear can weigh as much as 600 pounds (272 kilograms).

Russian families paint hard-boiled eggs **red**, **green**, and **yellow** for Easter. Easter is an important holiday in Russia. Families go to church on Easter Sunday. Then they eat the eggs and a special Easter cake called *kulich*.

Golden lights shine in Moscow. Moscow is the capital of Russia. Many families in Moscow live in apartment buildings. Two families sometimes share the same apartment.

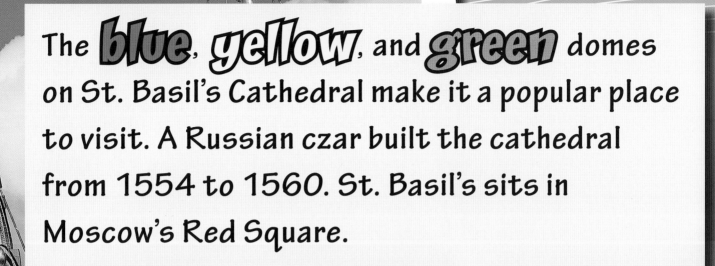

The **blue**, **yellow**, and **green** domes on St. Basil's Cathedral make it a popular place to visit. A Russian czar built the cathedral from 1554 to 1560. St. Basil's sits in Moscow's Red Square.

A **brown** fur hat covers a child's head. Fur hats help Russian people stay warm during the long winters. Many Russian children enjoy sledding down snowy hills in winter. They also like to ice skate on frozen ponds.

Russian farmers welcome spring by planting **orange** and **yellow** sunflowers. Russia produces more sunflower seeds than any other country in the world.

Russian schoolchildren in **red** uniforms laugh with friends at lunchtime. All kids in Russia attend school from ages 6 to 14. Many kids go to high school after that. Russian schoolchildren study reading, writing, math, science, history, music, and art.

Popular *matryoshka* dolls come in **purple** and many other colors. Russian artists paint the dolls by hand. Each wooden doll is filled with a smaller wooden doll. Some sets have more than 70 dolls inside!

The deep **blue** water of Lake Baikal lies in southern Siberia. It is the deepest lake in the world. At 25 million years old, Lake Baikal is also the world's oldest lake.

This **white** Arctic fox blends in with the powdery snow. Arctic foxes live in the Siberian tundra of northern Russia. In summer, Arctic foxes are brown. But in winter, they turn snow white.

Dancers in **green** and **white** costumes perform in a Russian ballet. Ballet has been a popular dance in Russia since the 1700s. Many of the world's best ballet dancers come from Russia.

Red borscht is one of the most popular foods in Russia. Borscht is a soup made of beets. Russians enjoy borscht with a large piece of fresh bread. They eat the soup cold in the summer and warm in the winter.

A **green** dacha shines in the sun. Dachas are Russian country homes. Families visit their dachas in the summer. Adults take care of the small gardens. Children play in the grass. Perhaps you will visit a dacha in Russia someday.

FACTS about Russia

Capital City: Moscow

Population: 140,702,096

Official Language: Russian

Common Phrases

English	Russian	Pronunciation
hello	privyet	(pri-VYET)
good-bye	dosvidanya	(dah-svee-DAH-nyah)
yes	da	(DAH)
no	nyet	(NYET)

Map

Flag

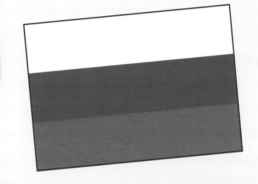

Money

Russian money is called the ruble. One ruble equals 100 kopeks.

Glossary

Arctic fox (ARK-tik FOKS) — a small fox that lives near the Arctic Ocean; the Arctic is the frozen area around the North Pole.

ballet (bal-LAY) — a performance that uses dance to tell a story

borscht (BORE-sht) — a soup made of beets

czar (ZAR) — an emperor of Russia before the revolution of 1917

dacha (DAH-cha) — a Russian summer home

Easter (EE-stur) — the Christian holiday on which people remember the death of Jesus

kulich (koo-LEECH) — Russian Easter cake

matryoshka (mah-TROOSH-kuh) — a set of wooden dolls; each doll fits inside a bigger doll.

Siberia (si-BIHR-ee-uh) — a large area of Asian Russia; Siberia has very long and cold winters.

tundra (TUHN-druh) — a cold area of northern Europe, Asia, and North America where trees do not grow; the ground stays frozen in the tundra for most of the year.

Read More

Sheen, Barbara. *Foods of Russia.* Taste of Culture. San Diego: KidHaven Press, 2006.

Spengler, Kremena. *Russia.* Questions and Answers. Countries. Mankato, Minn.: Capstone Press, 2005.

Internet Sites

FactHound offers a safe, fun way to find educator-approved Internet sites related to this book.

Here's what you do:

1. Visit *www.facthound.com*

2. Choose your grade level.

3. Begin your search.

This book's ID number is 9781429622257.

FactHound will fetch the best sites for you!

Index

A+ Books are published by Capstone Press,
151 Good Counsel Drive, P.O. Box 669, Mankato, Minnesota 56002.
www.capstonepress.com

1 2 3 4 5 6 14 13 12 11 10 09

Library of Congress Cataloging-in-Publication Data
Ipcizade, Catherine.
    Russia in colors / by Catherine Ipcizade.
        p. cm. — (A+ books. World of colors)
    Includes bibliographical references and index.
    Summary: "Simple text and striking photographs present Russia, its culture, and its
geography" — Provided by publisher.
        ISBN-13: 978-1-4296-2225-7 (hardcover)
        ISBN-10: 1-4296-2225-3 (hardcover)
        1. Russia (Federation) — Pictorial works — Juvenile literature. I. Title.
DK510.23.I63 2009
947 — dc22   2008034124

Credits
Megan Peterson, editor; Veronica Bianchini, set designer; Kyle Grenz, book designer;
    Wanda Winch, photo researcher

Photo Credits
Alamy/Bill Lyons, 15; Alamy/FocusRussia, 26–27; Art Life Images/age fotostock/
Alvaro Leiva, 8–9; Art Life Images/age fotostock/Sylvain Grandadam, 22; Art Life
Images/age fotostock/Wojtek Buss, 10; Capstone Press/Karon Dubke, 16, 25;
Courtesy of Svetlana Zhurkina, 29 (coins); Minden Pictures/Sergey Gorshkov, 2–3;
Shutterstock, 29 (banknotes); Shutterstock/AresT, 6–7; Shutterstock/Brian A. Jackson,
1; Shutterstock/Elena Yakusheva, cover; Shutterstock/nialat, 21; Shutterstock/poresh,
18–19; Shutterstock/Radlovsk Yaroslav, 4–5; Shutterstock/Sasha Davas, 29 (flag);
Shutterstock/Suzanne Tucker, 12–13

Note to Parents, Teachers, and Librarians
This World of Colors book uses full-color photographs and a nonfiction format
to introduce children to basic topics in the study of countries. *Russia in Colors*
is designed to be read aloud to a pre-reader or to be read independently by an
early reader. Photographs help listeners and early readers understand the text
and concepts discussed. The book encourages further learning by including the
following sections: Facts about Russia, Glossary, Read More, Internet Sites, and
Index. Early readers may need assistance using these features.